Success With Podcasts by Dominic Murray

Introduction: What Is a Podcast?

Podcasting is the process of preparing as well as distributing digital audio tracks. These files are then transferred to streaming and download services that the listener can play on their phones or digital media players. There are, in 2022, nearly two million podcast shows consisting of 48 million episodes, and growing.

Podcasts may seem to be a very twenty-first century phenomenon, yet their birth can be traced back to the latter part of the last millennium. Evolving from the birth of computer-based journals and early web-based opinion forums of the 1980s, podcasts were initially referred to as "audio blogging". In audio blogs, people shared their thoughts and experiences with others via recordings on cassettes. It took until the mid-1990s, and the popularised use of the World Wide Web for there to be an accessible method of sharing these audio blogs with other people. This inability to make these recordings available to the public was further reduced, when the combination of MP3 with RSS feeds allowed audio content to be more simply embedded into websites.

In the month of October 2001, 'Apple' released its first MP3 portable player. It was called the 'iPod'. Not only was the 'iPod' revolutionary to the music industry, it also became the first mainstream method of accessing and carrying about the audio blog. Then, in 2004 Adam Curry, a former 'MTV' employee and the software developer Dave Winer, created a programme called 'iPodder'. In allowing users to save audio blog posts on their 'iPod', 'iPodder' helped speed up the creation and sharing of audio blogs.

The trend was observed by British journalist Ben Hammersley who wrote extensively on the emergence of "online radio casting", and which eventually led to him using the term "podcasting", connecting the words "iPod" and "radio casting". Hammersley's word, created for sake of padding out an article written for the British newspaper, 'The Guardian', was now, or rather was to become, part of humanities social and technological history.

This book will help anyone wanting to be part of this global evolution in information sharing. Help build an idea for a podcast, purchase the correct equipment, plan episodes, produce shows, promote content and explain how to create a revenue from the podcast.

1: Why Podcasting Has Bloomed

The main benefit of podcasting is that it provides unlimited options and possibilities for discussions. Unlike the mainstream radio programming, any topic one might be interested in could be found on the internet as a podcast. From an authentic crime podcast to comedy podcasts, news, pop culture, or opinions, there's something for anyone. Moreover, aspiring podcasters can post details about their subject through podcast hosting platforms and quickly become part of this listening revolution.

An advantage of downloading podcast episodes is that the listener can use playback controls to set their own pace of listening and revisit parts of a show, interview or debate. Audio content from podcasts allows listeners to explore topics without setting aside time to read or view videos. That said, videos are becoming an advantageous addition to podcast production; more of that latter. Podcasts also feature content in smaller chunks, ideal for everyday commutes or hectic schedules. And, through a simple piece of planning and downloading a preferred programme or show, there is always something available for the ears.

This may be part of the reason why the format of podcasts has grown in popularity. A recent study found that in the United States alone, over 177 million people have listened to a podcast. The location in which they choose to listen divides as follows; 49% is done in the home environment, 22% of while driving, 11% at work, and 8% of listens while exercising. In 2021 the top five categories of podcasts were; Culture & Society, Comedy, Business, Health, as well as News and Politics.

By conducting often more frank and honest interviews than are permitted through more traditional style of media formats; television, radio and printed news, Podcasts provide deep dives into the thoughts of leaders in specific sectors, industries, political ideologies and movements or any number of topics. Indeed, the beauty of podcasts, or as they are increasingly being referred to, "pods", is there flexibility. This allows the audience of a pod to become experts in their favourite topics and for those with something to say to have those views or that information placed into the world.

With podcasting now being such a popular activity, more care must be taken in choosing the topic, name and how often the podcast is published. Studying the podcasting trends can help create an engaging and popular show. By analysing these statistics, the right decisions for success can be made. And, this may even lead to you being able to generate an income from your podcast show.

Podcast Listener Demographics

Who is listening to podcasts?

- 50% of the monthly U.S. podcast listeners are aged between 12 and 34 years, with 43% between 35 and 54 years old.

- The 26% of U.S. Americans who listened to weekly podcasts do so through an average of eight podcasts a week.

- In 2019, one survey showed that 22% of people who listen to podcasts listen to more than 22 hours of podcasts every week!

- The same report shows that 35% of people listen to at least ten programmes each month.

How Do People Listen to Podcasts?

According to Statista's 2020 study, the most popular platforms and applications for listening to podcasts are Spotify (25% of listeners) and Apple Podcasts (20%).

In 2019, 65% of users preferred to listen to podcasts through their smartphones, while 25% preferred desktop computers.

Why Do People Listen to Podcasts?

Learning about new topics is why 74% of listeners tune-in or download their chosen podcast. While others state that they are seeking entertainment, to "stay up-to-date", for general relaxation or get ideas.

Which Podcasts Are the Most Popular?

Of the new listener, the top podcast downloads are; Music, with Arts and Health & Fitness making up the top three most frequently downloaded topic areas. In comparison, regularly returning listeners to a podcast show are more interested in History, News, True Crime and Science.

Should My Podcast Use Video?

Despite the numerous advantages of launching a podcast with a video (more audience engagement and promotional opportunities) in 2019, only 17% of podcasters created an accompanying video. But with

Spotify now making video podcasts accessible to their subscribers this could be the USB (unique selling point) that your podcast requires.

Reaching Your Audience

Aim to reach the "super listeners". These are the people who will tune into more than 20 hours of audio content each week. This will make for an unstoppable fan base. But how does one create a "super listener?"

Get your show on the charts of the podcast download and listening app stores is the best method of making your show visible to a potential future listener. Do this by soliciting your current listener to subscribe to your podcast through your "intro" and "outro". This is your CTA or "call-to-action". And, obviously exploit your friends and family by having them click-on and download your podcast.

Upload your podcast to your social media platforms and collaborate with relevant influencers to help promote your podcast to their respective audiences. Join forces with other podcasters to promote each other's shows, and keep people coming back to your show by ensuring it is presented to the world with love, fulfils the entertainment needs and values of your "super listener".

If you have language skills, consider recording your podcast in a tongue other than English. While the USA, Sweden, Australia and the United Kingdom all continue to be atop the listener demographics, the podcast trend is showing momentum in Latin America and Africa.

So, if you have fluency in Portuguese, French or Spanish, try recording in those languages.

Most important of all, ensure that your show is recorded using a high-quality microphone and editing software. A third of listeners say that poor quality of podcasts is the main reason why they stop listening. So, if you want to bring listeners to your podcast and turn them into fans who will be talking with their friends about your pod, coming back each time you publish a new episode and contributing to your revenue through 'Patreon', or other crowdfunding sites, it is essential to pay attention to this last point.

Finally, before starting

Listen to some of the most popular podcasts within the topic or subject area in which you want to make your podcast. Through taking the time to do this simple piece of research you will develop an idea as to the tone and pace of delivery best suited to your chosen subject matter. It is also an excellent method of understanding who are your main shows of competition and thinking about what it is that you and your pod can offer the listener which those others do not.

2: Getting Started - Podcast Equipment

Once you've got an idea of where you want to take your podcast, it is time to look over your equipment requirements. The three items you'll require at a minimum are a microphone, a pair of headphones and some hardware into which you can store, edit and from which you publish your show; such as a laptop.

Microphones

A microphone will be required for yourself and an additional microphone for any guest which you plan to interview. There are many aspects to consider in selecting a microphone, like style and quality, as well as the price. For a quick start, the Blue Yeti and Audio Technical microphones, will get you going without breaking the bank. The internet is filled with reviews of microphones and there are some very instructive articles and YouTube videos which will explain the details of how condenser, USB, directional and omnidirectional microphones differ.

Here are a handful of the leading microphones used for podcasting; 'Rode Podmic', 'Blue Yeti', 'JLab Talk', 'Blue Yeti X' and the 'Elgato Wave'.

Headphones

Headphones are often overlooked, but they are essential to creating an excellent studio for podcasting. A quality pair of headphones allows you to ensure background noise has been eliminated from the recording.

Software

There are plenty of options in the realm of editing software for podcasts. The most suitable option for you is the one which you find most intuitive to use, as mastery of the software will be achieved all the quicker.

If you're new to podcasting, it is best to start with simple software, such as 'Audacity' or that 'Podcastle', which is part of the hosting company, 'Acast'. These are free to download.

Microphone Arm

You must purchase microphone arms if your guests wish to keep their microphones during the entire broadcast. Which certainly makes for a more fluid and natural sounding exchange of words. They are an essential component of any studio that produces podcasts. Arms for microphones are also seen as crucial because they ensuring an even sound throughout the entire podcast. A microphone arm will additionally help you and any interviewee feel more comfortable during the recording; feeling far less intrusive than having a stranger thrust a microphone at your face.

Shock Mount

A shock mount is typically built into a microphone arm. They help eliminate sound generated by impacts or vibrations with the microphone, the arm or the table to which the microphone arm is attached.

Pop Filter

A pop filter stops the loud pop sound caused by rapid-moving air hitting the microphone. Pop filters are the fabric layer put over or in front of the microphone. The most important thing is to ensure that the filter is big enough and can be set at various angles to stop all airflow towards the microphone. Other names for pop filters include "windscreens", or when you're using a microphone held by a hand, it could be referred to as a "foam ball".

Portable Digital Recorder

If you plan to record any podcasts during your travels, consider investing in a portable digital recorder. Of course, you could also make recordings using your smartphone. However, digital recorders will be more durable and offer a better-quality recording.

Audio Mixers

Mixers give greater control over the production of the podcast. With mixers, you can boost or reduce the volume of various frequencies and create an excellent podcast with the highest audio quality. Unfortunately, it isn't easy to understand how to use the mixer. For this reason, it may be that you hold off purchasing an audio mixer until you know that podcasting really is for you. However, it's a must-have tool for anyone serious about podcasting.

Audio Interface

You may have the best quality headphones, microphones, and software available, however, the recording will not reach the highest quality if affected by external sound interface. Therefore, it is essential to locate your recording studio or place in which interviews are to be held in a location or room which is as devoid of external noise interference as is possible. Poor quality sound recording is the number one reason that the listener gives for not engaging with a podcast.

3: Choosing Your Topic, Name and Length

Success with a podcast will usually come from it being a recording that has authenticity. That is going to derive from the host having command over the subject, or at least a genuine passion for the topic being covered.

There are many names that a podcast could take. Ideally the title for the podcast should be chosen in relation to its subject matter. If, you are a comedy performance then a fun, unique and imaginative name could be fitting. But in most instances, it is best to keep the title clear, on point and descriptive of the subject of the podcast. One thing is that the word "podcast" is redundant. Your listener knows that it is a podcast.

After settling on the subject and title, the length of the podcast should be the next consideration. Most podcasts, which are to be regular shows, are between 20 to 45 minutes and are published at least once a week. Should help be required in making these decisions, on subject matter, title and length, consider the following...

Imagine the Audience

Most people will want to begin recording a podcast because there is a subject matter or issue which is felt by them to be lacking as an option to the listener or it is an area in which the hosts have specialist knowledge or unbridled passions. The subject matter will typically give rise to a suitable name for your show, but if not then consider the listener.

Success in choosing the right name for your podcast will come through having a picture of your audience in your mind's eye. Their personality, what the person listening will connect with in terms of presenter tone and pod show name, and even the font and colours of the thumbnail used to display your show on the host site. One trick for achieving this is to imagine yourself in the mindset of the listener you are trying to reach; What are their names, what are they looking for, what's their favourite way of consuming podcasts?

Making sure your audience is at the centre of your plans will ensure that you come up with the name of your show that is engaging and connects with those for whom you are recording in the first place.

Select A Descriptive Title

Although a poetic or mysterious name might appeal to you, the more precise the title of your podcast, the better. Including in the title the subject matter, such as Politics, Finance or Health and Fitness, could well be a smart move. However, don't end there. What specific perspective will your programme tackle?

For instance, if you're planning to start an exercise or health and wellness podcast, is there a more specific term you can apply to describe the range of topics to be covered?

Perhaps you are going to discuss wild swimming, football or Pilates. The more efficiently your listener will be able to discover your podcast the better.

Think of Your Podcast Name as a Brand

It doesn't matter if it's an official corporate brand name show or the show is an individual venture, it's essential to treat your podcast professionally from the start, and this can be best achieved though thinking of the podcast as a brand. Consider the characteristics of your brand which you wish to highlight and strengthen. For example, the tone of the podcast which best fits your personal or, if it is a corporate show, the company's image and tone?

Easy to Remember

By ensuring that the podcast tile is relevant to the subject matter it will be a far more memorable name for the listener. Additionally, buy keeping the title less than 30 characters there's more likelihood the podcast will be placed in the "recommendations" section of any chosen hosting site.

Be Careful with Grammar

This is an important one. It is not a good idea to distract or deter potential viewers with annoying grammar errors, for example:

- Its vs. It's

- They're vs. There vs. They're.

- Too vs. To

- Then vs. Than

Simple mistakes and typos could make your podcast appear unprofessional.

Do Your Research

The next step is opening your preferred search engine and looking up other podcasts within your chosen niche. Before you choose the perfect name for your podcast, it's crucial to ensure that no one else has already used this name. The reality is that unless a podcast name is trademarked, there's no reason why two podcasts cannot be named the same. But it may cause confusion for your listener - which is never a good idea! Besides, you want your potential listeners to be able to locate your show and know that it is you.

Your Podcast Name in social media?

As part of the process of promoting and keeping in touch with your "super listener" and increasing your podcasts audience, it is a great idea to have a strategy for promoting not only the latest show, but also other tip-bits or news which may be of interest or relevance to your audience. This may also include having a website and written blog dedicated to you podcast. Such locations are useful for sharing pictures, amusing or revealing moments with your show guests or the video of each show (if chosen to record one).

Getting into SEOs

For most this will be a step too far in the process of naming your podcast, but it is worth mentioning, and it may indeed be something that you want to consider. Particularly if you have an intention to make money from your podcast.

It may be argued that SEO or search engine optmisation, is a crucial aspect of establishing your podcast's listenership. Therefore, make sure you have the title that incorporates the main keywords and points to your show's topic, subject matter or theme. For instance, if the planned show revolves around Star Trek and is called "Beam Me Up, Scotty", consider adding a subtitle, "A Star Trek Superfan Podcast". This will aid in making your show more visible through Google searches, as well as on Apple Podcasts and Spotify.

Help with Generating a Podcast Name

If you are still struggling to think up a name for your podcast but, have a clear idea of what topic or subject you will be discussing on your show, the perfect name could come from one of the many free name generators found on the internet. These include; 'Riverside Podcast Name Generator', 'BizNameWiz', 'BNG Podcast Name Generator', 'Crowdspring', 'Kopywrite Kourse', 'NameBoy', 'Portent Podcast Name Generator', 'SquadHelp' and more. Make use of any of these suggestions to get your creative juices flowing!

Podcast Name Trends

If even after having followed through the earlier procedures' it is still a struggle to come up with a name for your podcast, it maybe that the following show examples, making themselves heard in 2022, can help give inspiration.

1. How I Constructed This

Sometimes simplicity is the best. In this podcast, Guy Raz speaks with entrepreneurs to learn how they created successful companies. The name of this pod is clear and concise.

2. Crime Junkie

This cool podcast name is excellent as it thinks about its listeners. The show, a mix of diverse crime stories, is intended for those who love exploring or solving these intricate crime scenes. Also, the listeners to this podcast are, in fact, Crime Junkies.

3. This is American Life

This American Life is an online radio show that, as its name implies, covers all aspects of everyday life in America. It's brief, easy, and simple to search when you're searching for something relevant to American Life, making it a perfect name for the show.

4. The Daily

Easy to recall, The Daily is a catchy podcast name that works for this journalistic talk show. "Daily" informs viewers that new episodes come every day, and it is reminiscent of the daily news.

5. For the Purpose

There are two ways to think about the original name of this podcast. The first is that the podcast is about the importance of living a purposeful life. Or, it can be seen as Jay Shetty, the host, living his purpose by sharing his knowledge. The podcast was made to help others fulfil their mission.

6. The Happiness Lab

This tagline is entertaining however it conveys precisely what it is supposed. The podcast host is Dr. Laurie Santos, a professor. She has researched living a happier life, precisely the topic she discusses in this show. The listeners will be invited into her happiness lab as they listen to the show.

8. Serial

Sometimes, you only need one clever word to create the perfect name for your podcast! A serial can be used to refer to two meanings. The first is that the podcast itself is a serial as it is released in a set of episodes. And, then there is the subject matter of the pod, which contains stories about serial murderers.

9. Freakonomics

We enjoy the mix of two words: the word "freak" and "economics". The podcast is based on an article of the same title written by an economist and journalist telling various tales about how things work.

10. Potterless

The host of this podcast, Mike Schubert, had never read the highly acclaimed Harry Potter series. Like the title suggests, he was "Potterless". This podcast chronicles his journey from being a Potterless adult to engaging with fans about the book and film franchise.

To surmise, when launching your podcast, choose a name which resonates with your audience, conveys your show's subject matter and is simple to remember. You should also ensure your name is distinctive and aligns with your personal or your company's brand. And, remember, if you can, to keep SEO at the forefront of your mind. This will help make your podcast visible in search results to the targeted listener.

4: How to Record and Edit Your Podcast

With topic and title in hand, it is now time to start recording your first show. Home studio or office setups are ideal for recording podcasts. There is control over your environment with fewer distractions and it is possible to keep the equipment setup in place, saving time in those moments when a great idea for a pod strikes. Plus, home recordings sound more professional than one undertaken on the street or in a communal space. Unless, of course the remit of your podcast is to pick up external sounds and interview passers-by. In which instance the soundscape will be essential to your show.

A podcast which seeks this external engagement or occasionally takes to the road, can make use of a smartphone for its recordings. Use the Voice Memos app on an iPhone or the Voice Recorder app on an Android device to record conversations outside and transmit them to your computer for editing. Or, even easier, try 'The Podcast Host', which claims to be able to take your phone recorded show and return it to you ready to publish.

Software Needed for Recording a Podcast

Whether you record in your house or outdoors, it is still necessary to edit the show with software. This smooths out the sound of your podcast. Delivering that all important professional quality sound to the ears of your listener. Most commonly used by beginners to professional podcasters, is the free to download software, Audacity. It's compatible with Windows, Mac, and Linux systems.

Audacity is easy and accessible for users, but there are also other software; 'GarageBand' is widely used by podcasters and musicians alike. 'GarageBand' is the *de facto* recording and editing software for Mac. 'Adobe Audition', offers a host of unique features.

This subscription-based service is an absolute must for professional users (although it comes with a steep learning curve!). In addition to the well-known editing and recording programmes, lesser-known software such as, 'Hindenburg' and 'Pro Tools' offer professional-grade editing and are worth exploring.

Choosing the Best Microphone

It is best to just get started recording, and anyone with a laptop or smartphone can do this. But any serious podcaster should know more about the types of microphones available and what are the benefits to each.

Built-in Microphones

Found in a laptop of smartphone, a built-in mic is not specifically designed to record professional quality audio. Instead, think of these as a way to record your first few episodes before moving on to something more professional.

USB Microphone

Simple to use right from the beginning, the USB microphone can be connected straight to computers and they usually do a great job for the amateur podcaster.

Dynamic Microphones

This type of microphone is specifically designed to concentrate on your vocals. Being directional, they block out noises from the background. If you have several presenters, a couple of these connected to a mixer is the ideal solution.

Condenser Microphones

Regarded as the industry standard by experts, a condenser mic records natural sound. It can pick up quiet sound and allows you to capture multiple live presenters.

Editing a Podcast

The finest audio quality for podcasts usually requires some editing magic. It doesn't make for fascinating listening when presenters take a long pause to gather their ideas. Therefore, gaps in conversation are among the most frequent issues that the producer of a podcast will face.

It is also vital that a chosen file type is industry standard. The most widely used podcast hosting services like Apple and Spotify use either MP4A or MP3. If you decide to upload your show as an MP3 file, and it is not already present on your laptop or chosen editing hardware, installing a LAME encoder is required. This is available for both Windows and Mac users to download from 'Audacity'.

Choosing The Length of Truncation

Your waveform length should be shortened. The settings chosen should remove any audio lower than -20dB and should not be more prolonged than 2 seconds. Try making a slight adjustment to the settings and listening to the audio if at playback your audio shows jarring or just off. Again, 'Audacity', can be used to enhance your podcast with a fade in and out, normalise audio for constant audio levels, and eliminate background noise.

Save Some Time – Automatic Editing Software

A call recorder option has recently been added by 'Alitu'. This allows for the recording of an interview or for a co-hosted show to be conducted over the phone, using 'Zoom', 'Google Meets' or 'Microsoft Teams' etc., and then have it automatically cleaned up. Returning a recording which has had noise reduction and levelling imposed post the interview.

In addition, you can modify your recordings, add intros, outros, advertisements, or transitions using 'Alitu's' convenient episode builder, and then just export the finished programme. With all the built-in options for editing and automatically cleaning up your audio, 'Alitu' does come with a cost, but it may be worth the outlay, as the service offers much more than just podcast recording.

5: Before Publishing Your Podcast

Asides from ensuring that the recording is edited correctly and as close to a professional standard as can be achieved by either your skills or your wallet, the "intros" and "outros", of a podcast give it polish and character. In addition, they increase your show's value and assist you in competing with the other two million podcasts out there, vying for the attention of your listener.

The intros and outros can be whatever you wish to make of them, but most shows use a short voiceover with background music. Intros typically last 30 seconds but not more than one minute. They provide the podcast's name and a brief description of it and the host. Finally, outros are typically straightforward "thanks for listening" messages, calls-to-actions and directions on how to subscribe. Together, these components ensure that your show is professional, easy to access, and valuable to the listener.

What Goes into A Podcast Intro?

There's only one chance to make an impression; therefore, making the right impression is vital to creating an incredibly sleek and high-value experience that will convince your audience to take the time to subscribe and keep coming back for more. A well-crafted podcast intro along with the artwork of the podcasts cover is leading your listener towards what to expect from the show. The intro clarifies the reason for the podcast, introduces the presenter, and assists a listener in understanding the benefits that they will obtain through listening.

Here are some of the elements that each podcast's intro should have:

1. **Podcast name:** Add your show's name to let people know to what they are listening.

2. **Episode title:** Similar to an article in a newspaper, the title of your episode should be clear and informative and/or intriguing and entice the listener.

3. **Episode number:** This establishes a chronology that helps your listener find audio content, notes and transcripts on each episode.

4. **Names of hosts:** Introduce yourself and any co-hosts.

5. **Time stamps:** Are typically placed in the description accompanying the podcast, but could be added to the Intro. A time stamp is useful to a listener for finding or returning to particular parts of your show which was of specific interest or if the listener chooses to consume the pod in smaller parts.

What Goes into A Podcast Outro?

Your outro may not be as crucial for the overall success of your programme as your intro (many people are likely to end your show when they hear the music in the outro). Nevertheless, it's an essential element of an effective presentation.

You could use the same song as was used in your intro; however, this is the only part of the outro which is going to be the same as the intro. The outro is the moment to express your appreciation to your listener and request that they do something, also known as the "call-to-action". You could suggest they:

- Engage with the podcast through its presents on social media.

- Donate on your Patreon page to help support your show financially.

- Comment on or review your show.

- Purchase memberships, merchandise, or even courses through the podcast's dedicated website.

- Inform your listener when they will be able to download your next episode.

Some podcasts frequently alter their outro based on the requirements of their audience. For instance, they may change from a "like us on Facebook" outro to a "donate to keep us going" outro.

Tips For Sticking to Your Recording Schedule

1. Remember: You're Only Human

If you miss an episode, don't panic. Life throughs up all sorts of challenges. Perhaps your child became sick, or your guest was forced to drop out at the very last moment. The best way to deal with this is to describe the events during the next episode of your podcast. Your audience will understand.

2. Brainstorm a List of Topics

Becoming the best podcaster will be more achievable if you are armed with endless topics. So, note down every thought which might make an episode for your podcast. This process can also be enhanced through listening to other podcasts, which may ignite your imagination. Don't duplicate them, of course, but do you have the ability to take something you like and add your spin on it?

Or it may be that in conducting keyword research about your intended market, ideas are generated. Ask your listeners what they would wish to learn or hear about in upcoming podcasts, and have them communicate this through 'comments' and 'message boards' attached to the podcast's social media or website. If you have sponsors, ask them to suggest topics to discuss. Develop the habit of adding to the list of ideas, so that as the content is drawn down in created podcasts there are always plenty from which to work.

3. Create an Editorial Calendar

Once you've compiled the many podcast topics and reduced them to concepts that are likely to have the potential to create a great episode, it is time to develop a schedule. Many podcasters prefer to keep things easy by using Google Calendar (or, more straightforward still, using a paper calendar) to schedule publication dates. There exist many excellent tools for managing projects, including; 'Trello', 'Asana', and 'Notion'.

4. Before Publishing the First Episode?

Another vital aspect of the editorial calendar planning procedure is establishing the date your podcast will be live. Don't forget that even if you've got an episode ready to air, it doesn't mean you must immediately release it. If the podcast is not about news or current events, which would be time sensitive, it is a good rule of thumb to have at least three podcasts ready to go before going live with the first. This can ensure you have a sufficient buffer of time protecting against future issues around recording or the production process.

5. Guard Against Production Backlog

Another vital aspect of avoiding "pod-fading" is reserving time on your calendar to allow for production and its planning. Make sure to schedule every step of the process, which could include:

- The outlining and preliminary research for each episode

- Contact guests

- Set a date/recording schedule with your guests

- Finalise sponsors

- Recording day(s) for the episode

- Editing day(s) for the episode, including incorporate sponsored content

- Promote the show (on your website, newsletter, Facebook, Twitter accounts, etc.)

Make sure to consider the time each step will require. It might take several episodes to understand the length of time required to complete the production cycle for each podcast.

6. Batching Tasks Helps Save Time

One excellent method to accomplish more in a shorter amount of time is to group similar tasks in a batch. For instance, you could devote an hour or two one day for initial research and then brainstorm ideas for the upcoming episode.

Although a lot of the steps in the production and planning of podcasts depend on collaboration with other people (including guests), certain aspects of production for podcasts do lend themselves to batching options; Outlining the episode, Editing recordings, Sponsor pitching or the scheduling of social media promotional events. Determine which steps of your podcast workflow could be completed in batches, and then plan your workflow accordingly.

7. Have a Podcast Studio Setup

One approach to overcoming continuous podcasting obstacles is ensuring your equipment configuration is as simple as possible. If you're tempted to purchase a top-of-the-line video recording camera or the most potent state-of-the-art microphone you can find, consider the setup time you'd like to spend at the occasion of recording your podcast.

Although quality audio is *crucial* for an effective broadcast, it is not necessary to break the bank on the best technology available. Sometimes, a reliable, plug-and-play audio device can do the trick and doesn't complicate the recording process.

8. Minimise Editing Time

Many amateur podcasters plan to address issues which have arisen in recording through the editing process. But, attempting to "fix it during editing" could result in long editing sessions. In addition, the longer it takes to make an episode, the more likely you'll be in the midst of your next planned podcast's schedule, causing slippage in the show's publication dates. Instead, concentrate on the recording plan devised for each episode and record as tightly to this as possible. With time and practice errors made during record will occur less frequently and this will also aide in speeding up editing.

9. Automate Where You Can

Take advantage of the many tools now available to make the process of producing and publishing a podcast as simple as possible. Where you can automate a process, do so. The scheduling of guests using applications such as 'Calendly' or 'Acuity', is a simple example of automation.

Using 'Acast' for recording your show gives the option of using a built-in automated scheduling system. The process of scheduling your social media promotions can be streamlined using tools such as, 'Buffer', 'Later' or 'Hootsuite'. And, there are tools for marketing via email, such as 'Convertkit.'

Tags In Podcast Hosting Platforms

In the early days of podcasts, tags were essential in getting noticed. But today tags are not required. 'Apple' holds over 50% of the content uploaded as podcasts. Nothing within 'Apples' system pays attention to tags. It is therefore not worth the time to establish your podcast show in association to specific tags.

Tags In YouTube

It has already been spoken of that there is an opportunity to co-record your podcast episodes alongside a video. Asides from 'Spotify', the most likely location for hosting your podcast video is 'YouTube'. This is a site where tags are important. 'YouTube', or rather its algorithms, use both the description and title tags associated with your podcast video to sort and prioritise. The description can also be used to direct viewers towards the podcasts associated website, blogs, social media or sponsors supporting your podcast.

Finally… Publishing Your Podcast

Once you've got an episode of your podcast recorded, you need to make it available to the world. That involves listing you show with the most reputable directories. As mentioned, many times already, 'Apple Podcasts' consistently ranks in the top spot as the most well-known directory globally, although it is being aggressively challenged by 'Spotify', which is currently the second-highest. This guide will walk you through uploading your podcasts to these platforms and other popular platforms such as 'Google Play', 'Stitcher', and 'TuneIn'.

An MP3 file of your podcast and an RSS feed created by your hosts are required for your listener to get hold of your show. RSS feeds utilise a variety of standard web formats which provide information on metadata and content such as episode titles, author names, episode titles and descriptions. Various directories will have different requirements but the industry-wide standard, used by 'Apple' and 'Spotify', is based on an RSS 2.0 compatible feed and a hyperlink for a cover image that is a square (1:1) of at least 1400 by 1400 pixels, not exceeding 3000 by 3000 pixels. The server which hosts your podcast must be able to handle byte-range requests to stream the audio files.

Once you've published the podcast to the preferred directory, such as 'Apple' and 'Spotify', you'll need to "claim" the podcast to receive essential statistics on your podcast, such as how many listeners and downloads. These are the leading global directories:

1. Apple Podcasts

'Apple Podcasts' can be described as the largest directory of podcasts worldwide. It's been an essential player since its launch in 2005. It was formerly part of 'iTunes' but, due to its popularity for podcast hosting, 'Apple Podcasts' was rebranded as an independent service. It's one of the most important directories for podcasts. Some say you're not making a podcast if your podcast isn't included on 'Apple Podcasts'. That's how important 'Apple' is to podcasts!

2. Google Podcasts

'Google Podcasts' is the most effective and sole way to listen to podcasts via Google's platform. The service was launched in 2019. 'Google Podcasts' automatically scans the web to collect podcasts. The most significant benefit of this directory is that Google now shows podcast episodes on its search results, making your podcast more easily found.

3. Spotify

With 271 million active monthly subscribers, 'Spotify' is a massive platform for audio-based content. Recently, 'Spotify' purchased 'Gimlet Media' and 'Anchor' as a sign of their enormous investment in the podcast business. Don't miss out on getting your content in front of their active audience.

4. Stitcher

'Stitcher' was the preferred choice for 'Apple Podcasts' to use in making podcasts available to Android users. That was before 'Google' entered the world of podcasts. As a result, 'Stitcher' has built up a loyal user base who continue to use the app. So, you'll want to join them, too, regardless of whether you're registered on 'Google Play'.

'Stitcher' also provides various tools for analysis to help assess how your show performs. However, remember that this information pertains only to the performance of your podcast on 'Stitcher'. It does not provide information on its performance on other platforms. Another great aspect of 'Stitcher' is that it is included in over 50 vehicle models, working in all vehicles with 'CarPlay' from 'Apple' and, 'Android Auto'. Therefore, 'Stitcher' is a must if you want your customers to have access to a simple method of listening to your podcast while travelling in their vehicle.

5. Podchaser

'Podchaser' is a vast library of podcasts. Members can rate and review episodes individually to help other users find new content. Each podcast is given an online profile that allows everyone to look up the episodes, details on the podcast's creators, ratings of the show, statistics, and much more. 'Podchaser's' listeners also appreciate their categories and list features. With each feature, users can sort by their preferences to find shows that match their preferences and then build lists of preferred episodes.

6. TuneIn

'TuneIn' is technically a multi-channel global radio station however, it's growing in popularity for podcast listeners, especially those who enjoy news, talk radio, and sports-related content. The platform has a listener base of 75 million, so you should never overlook it. It's worth listing your show on 'TuneIn', even if you don't think your audience is similar to its listener demographics. A major reason for doing so is because 'TuneIn' is from where Amazon's "Alexa" takes "her" audio-related content.

7. Pandora

'Pandora' is another well-known streaming site that comes with a practical recommendation algorithm. In August of 2019, 'Pandora' launched 'The Podcast Genome Project'. The project provides personalised podcast recommendations for each user. This is so specific that it works down to the level of the episode. It functions through monitoring a listener's "likes", "dislikes" and listening histories.

8. Overcast

'Overcast' is a no-cost podcast player for 'iPhone', 'iPad' and 'Apple Watch' devices. A potential listener may prefer 'Overcast', because instead of algorithmic charts, members of 'Overcast' "star" their favourite shows to be added to the "Featured Podcast" section. With this service, listeners can sign up for a new podcast with just two clicks from the application. It's among the most accessible subscription processes available. The "Smart Speed" feature removes silent moments and dead air from podcast episodes. Another significant feature that is worth mentioning is "Voice Boost", which normalises the volume of an episode, ensuring that audio levels are equal from one show to the next. Say goodbye to eardrums being blown out!

9. Downcast

'Downcast' is another player for podcasts that works with 'Apple' products. 'Downcast' offers more features than 'Overcast', such as saving episodes in the cloud and advanced categorisation of episodes. 'Downcast' comes at a small cost, but comes with 'CarPlay' technology and the ability to stream shows via 'Chrome Cast'.

10. Learning Out Loud

If your podcast is targeted at the educational sector, an appropriate directory is 'Learn Out Loud'. An excellent resource for learning while on the go, this podcast directory is among the most extensive catalogues of free audio-first education resources.

11. Laughable

'Laughable' is the most effective way to listen and find comedic podcasts. Subscribers can join comedians and receive notifications when they launch the latest episode or are featured on a different podcast.

12. Acast

'Acast' boasts of having "all the world's podcasts" in their application. Offering free and premium versions, each can seamlessly communicate recommendations to your acquaintances using the "Nearby" feature.

Amazon Echo

Once your podcast is listed on the leading directories such as 'Apple', 'Google' or 'TuneIn'. Podcasts on these directories will be accessible via 'Amazon Echo'. These are activated using the "Alexa" voice activated interface. Expand the reach of your podcast by registering within "Flash Briefing". Then when every new episode is listed, your listen will be informed.

Cost to Make a Podcasts?

Podcasts can be published without cost through using a no-cost plan. Most podcast directories offer free plans, but for only a few dollars a month one can gain additional advantages.

That's a Wrap!

Bam! In a flash, your podcast has been featured in the best directories around the globe. Now, you can focus on creating engaging and valuable content for your expanding audience and watch your listener numbers rise. When your podcast is gaining traction, keep this trend going through using practical marketing tools and by adding exciting features such as live streams, live Q&As, and live chats with your listener.

6: Obtaining More Listeners

You've started your podcast and created some episodes. You are now trying to figure out how to increase the number of people listening to your podcast. Of course, every podcaster pays attention to this issue at some point in time. Except for a few instances of overnight success with your podcast, there are no shortcuts to increasing listenership.

The process requires understanding the key tasks which go into adding to your audience and remaining faithful to those steps. As with anything else in life, consistency wins out.

Submit Your Podcast to All Apps and Directories

This is an essential. Making absolutely sure that your show is available everywhere will obviously increase the likelihood of people discovering and listening to your podcasts. The first step is to upload your podcast's RSS feed to each podcast directory that you can locate. At the least ensure that your podcast is placed with 'Apple Podcasts', 'Google Podcasts' and 'Spotify', since they are the top three directories globally.

Don't stop there. Many smaller platforms are used each day. It is a surprisingly easy process and directories such as 'Acast' will take most of the hard work out of submitting to multiple hosts and even help with the process of monetising your pod!

Aim for Your Target Group

You might want to make an all-inclusive podcast, however, shows with an enormous sweep of appeal can be challenging to develop. So first, look at the most popular shows that appeal to you. It is usual that the producers or hosts already had an audience of significant size before beginning their show. That may have been from their work as print or television journalists, because they are famous for their past sporting success, have high social media profiles (influencers) or are knowledgeable about a particular lifestyle or business sector.

Assuming that you are not already well known by the broader public, listening to these more popular podcasts, using them to identify and understand your target audience is a very good approach when aiming at growing listenership.

A fabulous example of a podcast which began very small and is now widely listened to, is called, "Growing Up Halal". The hosts and producers identified that there were females of the broader Muslim community who feel that they are underrepresented. By targeting this very specific group in society the hosts have given themselves scope to speak broadly on geopolitical issues or at the more mundane level of daily survival and household chores.

Adding Video to Your Podcast

Making a video recording of your podcast at the time of recording and adding this to the 'Spotify' directory or onto 'YouTube', has been spoken of a great deal in earlier chapters. But it is worth reiterating that this is a trend only likely to grow. Perhaps thinking of this from different angles; adding cartoon imagery or even photographs and other graphics to illustrate the specifics under discussion within your podcast. Many people prefer video, and this means it is possible to reach more people by including videos of your show.

Be Part of The Community of Podcasters

Aside from becoming a guest of other relevant or cross-over pods, there are other ways to get your name and that of your show, on the map. Taking opportunities to participant in the wider podcast community or your shows particular niche is one such way. This might be through involving yourself in social media groups and discussions ('Facebook', 'Club House', 'TikTok' and others) or through joining groups which are relevance to your show and which exist in the physical world.

The objective is to deliver value to those discussions and groups. In the process, creating an attractive personality and demonstrating your authority on a subject or topic which is covered by the podcast that you host, produce and publish. Make sure to mention your show when appropriate but, don't become an unrelenting self-promotional spammer. That will do far more harm to your brand (be that personal or business) and having people vowing never to tune into your show. Rather the opposite of the desired effect!

Create A Podcast Trailer

A trailer can be a simple method of enticing people to listen to your show. It is much more appealing for people to listen, or even watch a trailer, before putting their energy into an entire episode. However, unless it's a comedy show and you have something particularly funny to share, which works out of context, you should not simply use a single snippet of a previous podcast episode. It is far better to create something unique that will help sell the worth to the listener of your show.

You could, for instance, create a montage. Including an introduction to yourself (or host if this is not you), explain what the podcast is about, then give snippets of your most popular guests and engaging segments from past episodes. Once armed with the trailer, publish it on your social media, pin it in your blog post, website or have it played by another podcast.

Create A Contest or Give Away

Giveaways are among the oldest methods that you can employ for creating buzz. People enjoy free things and are willingly to go through hoops to receive them. But be aware that people may engage with you just to win the reward, and aren't likely to stay as long-term fans. Therefore, you must ensure that you get something from them, like reviews.

You can announce a giveaway during your programme. Inform your listeners that all they need to do is write reviews (hopefully favourable) on your 'Apple Podcasts', 'Google Podcasts', and 'Spotify' page. Then, choose a random winner from all the reviews left. Reviewers might not be listening to every episode of your show, however, they will most likely be tuned in to hear the announcement of the competition winner. And, their comments will run for the rest of time.

If you use this method, announce your giveaway on social networks. Advertisements can be purchased to boost the impact of your competition announcement. The objective is to bring as many current non-listeners to participate in the contest. With luck, they will be captivated by your podcast and find it unthinkable to continue their lives without your show being part of it.

Be Serious About Using Social Media

Many podcasters commit the error of being lazy with social media. They will post something every time the next episode becomes available but do not make use of their social media profiles outside of this period. If you make use of social media correctly, you will be able to create lots of buzz around your podcast. Multiple posts through the week, or even the day, won't annoy your fans and listener, rather it will demonstrate to them how engaged you are with the subject matter on which you are posting. These tips will help you improve your social media skills:

- Teaser will promote upcoming episodes before they are aired. Creating excitement for each episode. This also allows for the promotion of existing content.

- Make sure you use a hashtag that is branded to promote your content. It allows your followers to participate in the discussion. In addition, those listeners and fans will help build buzz for your brand!

- Add hashtags related to the topic to each podcast.

- Use 'Facebook', 'Instagram', 'TikTok' and 'YouTube Shorts' to promote your show.

- Tag your favourite celebrities, organisations, artists, leaders, films, politicians, sponsors or other information which feature in your podcast.

- Post your message in pertinent 'Facebook' or 'Reddit' groups.

- Comment on the comments! Why not transform one of your "super listeners" into the role of an ambassador by engaging them and asking them to help out with your pod.

- Utilise enticing snippets from your show to create social media posts. You only need to write a few explanatory sentences and attach them to the snippets which will act as audiograms.

- Along as it is engaging, share non-episode-related content. These could include parts of interviews that didn't make it to the final show, behind-scenes highlights, or your thoughts and views on your niche or topic.

Get Your Podcast Website in Order

Although your listeners primarily consume your content using their preferred listening apps, your podcast's website is still a meaningful way to expand your podcast's listenership. A website is useless if nobody can locate it. Therefore, making your site available to interested listeners is crucial. So, take SEO seriously.

Creating a separate web page on your podcasts website for each episode allows for the sharing of show notes, the transcript and relevant links. This is written material that search engines will love.

The podcast might be secondary to your company and being produced in order to promote that brand. If that is the case then dedicate an area of your company website to the podcast. Make sure that there's ample functionality to frequently update new content.

Invest in Email Marketing

Once your podcast website is ready and functioning, you can use it to gather email addresses. Add a sign-up box and use call-to-actions on social media which direct to the podcast's website to gather your followers' email addresses. Once you've got this information, you can utilise the most efficient method of communication available to companies: email marketing.

Many podcasters use emails to inform their followers about new podcast episodes. It's a valid and legitimate usage and one you must consider doing. However, that's not all you can accomplish using email marketing. Use email marketing to keep in touch with your target audience. Do not be afraid to go beyond your show's realm to provide your viewers with relevant information. Suppose that your podcast is about true crime. In that case, it's perfectly acceptable to introduce your subscribers to a brand-new real-life crime 'Netflix' show which you think they'll like, even if you don't profit from the promotion.

It's impossible to build an email database using 'Gmail' (not without breaking the law and terms of use). Therefore, an email marketing application is a must. Some of the more familiar ones include; 'Mail Chimp', 'Drip' and 'ConvertKit'.

Conduct Interviews

There's a reason why interview shows are popular. Every interview exposes your show's content to a new demographic or character of viewer. The guest will, most likely, advertise their appearance in your programme to viewers, which will help promote your show at no cost. In this way, every episode can be considered a marketing asset.

These guests don't need to be celebrities. Ideally, they must be able to boast some fame, achievement or significant knowledge. However, you can include any person with an exciting story to tell. It could be experts, friends, or even someone engaging which through 'Twitter' or 'LinkedIn'. Make sure they've enough to talk about, and their content adds value to your listeners' life.

To get the most out of a featured guest ensure that every guest receives a mini-press pack that contains at least:

- Social media copy, photos, and videos, which include at least one picture of both your faces

- Your custom podcast artwork/logo.

- Intriguing quotes, clips, or timestamps from an episode.

- An accessible and unique hyperlink that can be tracked to your podcast's website (so you know the amount of traffic they generated for you).

- The hashtags and tags you would like them to include in the show's promotion.

If you provide all you can, they will discover that promoting your show will be easy and painless, increasing the likelihood that they'll do it.

Write A Compelling Podcast Description

A podcast description is often an unnoticed element when launching a new show. Many podcasters throw anything into the description box to get the chore over. However, this is one of the primary details that potential listeners will use to determine whether they want to check out an episode. Therefore, creating an engaging description that will entice listeners is essential.

Your description should be easy to understand. You might want to write several descriptions and then test them with friends before committing. Ensure you include the keywords people will search for to find shows similar to yours. Add information that will attract listeners, such as your credentials, the names of guests, and other specifics which the listener of your subject matter is likely to seek out.

Become A Podcast Guest

A simple way to introduce your podcast to potential listeners is to be a part of other podcasts through being their guest. Being a natural at interacting with people could be one of your most efficient marketing assets. To be invited to shows, other hosts need to believe that you have something valuable to offer their guests. Demonstrate that you can communicate effectively by engaging with the other podcast host and their production team though social media and, if an available option, through telephoning them direct.

If you don't get invitations naturally, creating a strategy for promoting your podcast which includes contacting other shows may be necessary. Look for shows that have audiences similar to yours. You can also use online services such as 'Interview Valet' or 'Club House' to secure interviews. Create a pitch that describes your background, the things you offer, and why you'd be a great guest. Include information on how you plan to pitch the episode from your side.

When you are invited to a show, mention your podcast! You're not being rude by making mention of your podcast and brand. Afterall, that's why you're there. Inform the audience about the best place to find you ('Apple Podcasts', 'Spotify', 'Google Podcasts' etc.), and how they could interact with your show (website and social media).

Buy Some Advertisements

A lot of the strategies for promoting your show take time. They can be effective but most likely not immediately. Paid for advertising on other podcasts can be a simple method to reach new listeners. Ensure that the podcast on which the advertisement is placed is similar to your own. This will mean that the audience is overlapping and thus far more likely to become permeant listeners of your podcast. You can quickly discover similar shows by browsing podcasts' directories or using a research tool such as 'SparkToro'.

Remember that viewers must hear about your programme multiple times before checking it out. This is known as the "simple exposure effect". Buy advertisement space for at least four shows, otherwise you won't receive enough exposure to have a positive impact. Additionally, you can buy 'Google' or 'Facebook' advertisements. Both provide different targeting options to identify people interested in your podcast's topic.

Consider Podcast SEO

Because podcasts are audio-based, they are not easy to consider in terms of SEO. However, certain elements, such as your episode title, are essential. Potential listeners will be searching for episodes of interest to them through podcast directories or listening apps. In that case, the title of an episode is an essential factor in search results. So, make sure you meet these following requirements when naming your episode…

- Include the details of guests and topics or events that you think your listeners would be interested in.

- Be descriptive and persuasive. It's alright to be a bit intriguing to get people to pay attention, but you should avoid obvious "clickbait".

- Use terms and phrases which your viewers regularly search for to locate a particular episode type.

- Avoid using generic titles that aren't meaningful to the listener, for example, "The Young Entrepreneur Podcast #37". It's not a good idea. Make use of subtitles to give more description and content meaning to searches.

Create A Marketing Process

This last tip about increasing the number of podcast listeners is the most crucial. There are many ways to market your podcast online. Therefore, it's essential to develop a process to follow every time you publish an episode. This will ensure that each episode receives maximum exposure. It is also the way to ensure consistency in your workflow so that no steps are overlooked.

Once you've refined your marketing workflow and transformed it into a reliable procedure, it can be transferred to others. This will become important once your podcast begins generating income and is therefore beneficial to employ an assistant to handle the specifics of promoting your show.

Here's an overview of the basic workflow for marketing. Once an episode is ready to be published:

- Make three 'Facebook' posts, ten 'Twitter' tweets along with six 'TikTok' or 'YouTube Short' posts about and between each episode of the podcast.

- Create videos, graphics, and audiograms for each blog post and which can be shared on the podcasts website and social media.

- Send mini press packages to guests.

- Published to the podcasts website the transcript and show notes.

- Contact friends and colleagues who may be interested in sharing the podcast and its associated promotion material.

- Create copy and images to share with your subscribers and email marketing list.

- Include the most recent episode in the signature of your podcasts email address.

Your workflow will not always be identical, but that's not a problem. Include and eliminate any components that you think suit a specific episode. It is vital to convert the marketing of your podcast into a repeatable process that can be quickly executed or delegated to other individuals.

Following these steps and the advice in this chapter will help ensure for an excellent podcast that has high-quality content and a sound growth plan. Then, with a bit of work your podcast's listenership should be consistently increasing.

7: Making Money from Your Podcast

Podcast sponsorships can be a potent marketing tool for brands and individuals alike. Being a potentially efficient monetisation method that is an excellent option for those who publish podcasts.

Connecting with brands you genuinely appreciate allows you to make money from the podcast while maintaining a real connection with your listeners. With the assistance of a podcast sponsor, you can make money from your show, expand your reach and create long-lasting partnerships with various brands. Before you begin looking for your first sponsor, you must understand how advertising in podcasts works.

Advertisement Format

Podcast sponsors, also known as advertisers, will pay to promote products or services on podcast episodes. There are two principal methods to advertise, "radio-style" or "host-read".

Radio-Style Ads

This format is where an outside marketing firm creates advertisements, and you then place them within your podcast. And, according to 'Edison Research', 70% of listeners are influenced to purchase the product after hearing of it on their favourite podcast. So, if you were wondering if radio-style adds were effective, the answer is a definite yes!

Host-Read Ads

Instead of placing an advertisement the podcast host or production team write about the service or product and the reasons why it is beneficial to them. In creating the story be sure that it is natural and flows. Host-read ads are the most well-known choice, accounting for more than 63% of podcast advertisements.

Where To Position an Ad

Whatever option you decide to go with, take into consideration the following three locations for ad placement:

- Pre-rolls: right before the show begins

- Mid-roll: somewhere in the course of the podcast. Mid-roll advertisements are among the most expensive for advertisers to purchase. This is due to the listener engagement usually being at its highest in mid-episode.

- Post-rolls: After the show. Post-roll advertisements are not as popular with advertisers because there is a tendency for lower engagement towards the conclusion of episodes.

How much advertisement time per episode?

Advertisements taking up more than 10% of the episode's total length could backfire; turning off your listener. Instead, try to include 30 to 60-second advertisements for services and products that will benefit or interest your listener.

Receiving Sponsorship

The requirements for receiving sponsorship will differ from brand-to-brand, but the level of sponsorship is typically associated to the number of downloads achieved by each podcast.

Some models aren't practical unless your podcast has an audience of thousands. In contrast, others work even with the attention of a couple of hundred people. Consider these questions before looking for sponsorship:

- Do I always get at least 200 downloads for each episode?

- Have I done my best to establish trust with my target audience?

- What services or products would bring value to my audience?

Ways To Find Podcast Sponsors

The method you employ to present to brands is largely contingent upon the volume of listeners associated with your podcast and the target audience of the potential sponsor. Here are four primary ways to approach potential sponsors.

1. Pitch Directly to The Brands

This is the best choice for podcasters who don't want to share their future sponsorship earnings with a media company or podcast network group. The media company would work on behalf of your podcast and in return for finding sponsors take an agreed percentage of the revenue. Through doing the leg work yourself and meeting with companies to pitch your show directly, more of the sponsorship cash will come directly into the coffers of the podcast.

This technique allows for the creation of mutually beneficial partnerships that avoid network splits and gives total control over the partners associated with your podcast. It's not easy to pitch your podcast to companies. Taking time, a thorough knowledge of the various advertising models, and strong negotiation skills will be imperative if choosing to take this route.

2. Join A Podcast Network

Ideal for Podcasters with 5,000 to 10,000 plus downloads per episode. A podcasting network will undertake finding sponsors, so you can concentrate on producing content. Of course, the podcast network business is looking to take a portion of the advertisement revenue, this is usually about 30%.

3. Use A Podcast Advertisement Marketplace

Podcast advertisement marketplaces connect companies seeking to purchase advertisement space with podcasters. Through them brands can search numerous shows to locate one that is an ideal fit. Marketplaces will earn between 10% and 30% from your sales. If considering this path, here are some marketplaces to consider contacting:

Podcorn

'Podcorn' is an ad-based marketplace that uses an affiliate model, which makes it a fantastic choice for all podcasters, regardless of the number of downloads. Their self-service platform for sponsorships of podcasts assists independent creators in identifying affiliates they can authentically endorse. 'Podcorn' allows a podcaster to retain more earnings as it takes only 10% of the income from your ads.

Buzzsprout

If you run your podcast on, 'Buzzsprout', take advantage of the offered affiliate marketplace. It will open up advertising income through a variety of brands, and is open to podcasts regardless of the number of recorded listeners.

Anyone who is a 'Buzzsprout' podcaster can become an affiliate of these brands, receive a payment in cash and retain the entire amount they earn. Look through the marketplace for companies you believe will resonate most with your target audience and complete the form for affiliates. You should receive a reply within a few days.

Gumball

'Gumball's' marketplace functions are similar to 'Podcorn' but operates on a CPM (cost per mille) model. Companies and brands can set filters to search for podcasts on which they wish to purchase hosts-read advertisement.

AdvertiseCast

'AdvertiseCast' is a network of podcasts featuring more than 1,500 shows in its catalogue. To become a member of 'AdvertiseCast's' marketplace, the podcast must be an affiliate of the network. This carries specific influencer requirements.

Acast

Acast is a network of podcasts and an advertisement marketplace. Podcast hosts can work with the creators of 'Acast' to develop original advertisements which appeal to their show's listenership. The hosts read the ads and place them where they want within the episode. Anchor's CPM rate is $15.00 (£13.00), which is paid on an episode-by-episode basis.

Anchor

'Anchor' sponsorship works with podcasts which are hosted with them. The service helps podcasts match with the right sponsors. Through it one can add messages from sponsors to your archive. Payment to the podcast is made when episodes reach 1,000 listens. The great part of this is that it is accumulative so, older episodes are included.

4. Use Affiliate Marketing

Ideal for podcasts with a smaller audience. With affiliate marketing a podcast is paid per sale. Which is typically made through the listener using a link. Affiliate marketing is among the most efficient way to find your first advertising or sponsorship partner.

The top podcasting affiliates are:

- 'Amazon Associates'

- 'Audible'

- 'Skillshare'

- 'Buzzsprout'

- 'BarkBox'

Podcast Advertising Models Explained

Before signing a contract with a company, it is crucial to know to what you are sign-up and how it may benefit your podcast. The three most important advertising models currently used with podcast advertising are:

CPM

The best for Podcasters with more than 10,000 subscribers, CPM is the abbreviation for "cost per mille". It represents the fact a podcast will only be paid by an advertiser for every 1,000 listens that the advertisement receives. The majority of podcast CPM rates paid are around $20.00 (£16.00). So, to generate $100 (£88.00) a podcast would need to have had 5,000 downloads of an episode. This advertising model can be lucrative for popular podcasts but isn't a good fit for many independent or smaller podcasters.

Affiliate Model (CPA)

The CPA or "cost per acquisition" model suits new podcasters or those struggling to increase download numbers. It works through compensating the podcast for every sale made using the affiliate hyperlink. The affiliate model is ideal for podcasters with an engaged audience. A good rule of thumb for this model of revenue generation is to assume that one percent of your show's listenership will respond to an advertisement. With an average commission rate of 15%, it is then possible to calculate the probable earnings for your podcast.

Value-Based

If your listener is actively engaged with your podcast then this approach may suit. With this method companies pay a fixed fee to promote their product or service through your podcast. With 200 listeners a podcast can make $500.00 (£440.00) from a single product mention. Compared this to the $4.00 (£3.50) for an average CPM rate for the same audience number.

Giving quality to companies and brands is the key to success through this approach. It's possible that you don't have many listeners, but companies will be taking notice of your podcast if your podcast has a handful of enthusiastic and engaged fans.

A Quality Pitch Will Bring Advertising Partners

When approaching potential advertising partners, it is a great idea to be fully prepared. Part of this will include an information pitch deck and a media pack, which could include details such as:

- A brief description of your podcast

- Your audience demographics

- A pitch deck with clips and promotional information

- An explanation of why podcast advertisements will work for the company being pitched to and also your podcast

- Contact details

Don't lose confidence in your pitch. Once you have presented to a company or brand, wait a week and if nothing comes of it be ready with an encouraging and polite follow-up email.

8: After the Podcast

When the Covid-19 pandemic hit and most people were restricted to their homes many took up podcasting to pass the time. Between March and the end of April 2020, more than 49,000 new podcasts had been published in America. Reported listening of podcasts also increased by 20% between March and April 2020.

Fast-forward to mid-2021, and the evidence indicates that following a subsidence in the outbreak there has been a slight reversal in these podcast trends. Nonetheless, podcasts have become a preferred form of entertainment. And, for any new or aspiring podcast host or producer, it is worth being cognisant that now more than ever it is crucial to market and promote your podcast.

Basic Podcast Promotion Tactics

Your First Episode

Be attentive to your first episode, and consider creating a "Trailer" episode which can be made available to help people understand about your podcast. It is also worth following these recommendations:

- With most directories there are "New Listener" sections. There a new podcast will be easily located by a listener.

- Record a brief trailer and elaborate on the idea and background of the show's concept in the initial episode.

- Record your trailer when you've completed at least 3 episodes of your podcast.

Stay Ahead with Your Publishing

In addition to the initial three episodes, it's an excellent idea to have three additional episodes completed. This relieves the stress when you launch your podcast and its associated marketing campaign. This approach gives peace of mind and time to focus on advertising and promoting your podcast.

Invest In Basic Marketing Materials

If launching a podcast is more than just a casual interest and intended to be a long-term undertaking, which may even bring in significant income, it is necessary to approach podcasting as a career.

Just as with a new business, it is worth having business cards, a logo, website, 'LinkedIn' and social media in place. Artwork and designs can be made at an affordable rate through online third-parties such as, 'Fiverr', '99 Designs' or 'UpWork'. The chosen designer should also design 'Facebook', website page and 'Twitter' page headers and other social media PR materials to use on the internet and in print.

Word Of Mouth

The power of word-of-mouth isn't to be underestimated. Especially when just starting out. Contacting old acquaintances to inform them of your podcast venture can give an incredible boost to your project. In addition, depending on the subject of your podcast, you could also talk to your co-workers, family members, virtual meetups, and social media groups within your area of expertise.

Engage With Your Guests

When you have guests to the podcast ask them to provide you with links to their social media accounts, books they're promoting, a brief biography and profile photographs. This will ensure that an appealing guest section, with pictures and hyperlinks to their work is available to the interested listener.

Reviews Are Important

Reviews remain crucial and should not be left out. They provide credibility and social evidence to the podcast.

9: Conclusion

Podcasting is most certainly a medium that is trending. The reasons for this are various. Podcasts are both a means of imparting your views and developing a deeper insight into others. They allow anyone to inform the world of their passions and specialist knowledge and in return give others the opportunity to delve into sometime obscure subjects, and perhaps, become experts of particularly obscure topics.

Then there is the practicality of podcasts; easy to carry about with you and no more obtrusive than is a modern smartphone. Giving anyone, constant access to knowledge or their favourite comedian or political thinker. Podcasts are changing the world, and it is the hope of the author that podcasts will be part of humanities awaking to new ideas. A cultural and political learning which may galvanize positive change in the world.

In there more crude form, podcasts are then, an extraordinary instrument, capable of showcasing incredible people and ideas. And, an extraordinarily handy marketing tool for both companies and individuals.

For anyone hoping to begin an effective podcast, it is hoped that the words of advice and tips contained within this book are the start of your journey towards having a fruitful, and maybe profitable, experience with podcasting.